MONEY HOW MUCH IS ENOUGH

MONEY HOW MUCH IS ENOUGH

A Guide to Help You Secure Your Future

William T Gillion, Sr

Copyright © 2019
William T Gillion, Sr.

All rights reserved

ISBN:9781796515220

This publication is designed to provide accurate and authoritative information regarding the subject matter covered. It is sold with the understanding that the writer is not engaged in rendering professional services. If professional advice or other expert assistance is required, the services of a competent professional person should be sought.

Introduction

THE REASON FOR THIS BOOK

We talk a lot about educational opportunities in America, but the fact is that America is far behind many countries in this world.

As I view the lives of Americans, I see that we live in the greatest land of opportunity in the world and yet we do not know how to take advantage of the opportunities we have.

I watch children when they are born and, in a few months, they are filled with questions. Everything around them is a mystery and they are busy searching for answers. If you continue watching them you will see how creative they are. They will find a way to do almost anything they choose to do.

By the time they are ready for school, they are busy talking, searching, and finding answers.

But the first thing they are told in school is that we do not talk unless we are asked a question, we do not look for answers, they will be told what they can and cannot do. They are required to stop thinking for themself and that they will be told what to do.

Don't get me wrong, they must learn to work and play as a team, but if they don't give in soon; they are put on medicine to control them and break their will.

Many children find something to do in class because they are so far ahead of the other class members, "they are bored."

By the time they graduate, they have been broken and are no longer able to think on their own and must be told by someone else what and when to do things.

There are about 2% of the children that survive school and still have a creative spirit in them. They are the ones that can see ideas and see value in things that others do not see. They become our leaders and hold top positions because they can still think for themselves.

This is where our inventors come from.

I think it is strange that only about 2.5% of Americans are in the upper-income group that can earn 100,000.00 dollars or more.

We encourage our youths to go to school and get an education so they can get a good job, but many graduate from high school, and if you ask them what their plans are they will say I guess I will get me a job, or they will say I guess I will go to college. When you ask the ones that say I will get a job, what type of job do you plan to get, they don't have any idea. When you ask the ones that say they are going to college, they don't know what they want to do or to study.

Even though many of our schools are doing a good job, I find it strange that high school and college graduates do not know anything about finances or even how to balance a checkbook.

I know that you can study finance if you choose to work in this field, but everyone will need to be able to handle their finances. Many young people ruin their credit ratings because they don't know how to protect them.

I also think it is strange that many businesses are started by people that did not graduate. This sometimes is a blessing because many times the things we learn keep us from being successful. We have to forget many things we learned and learn many things that we never learned to be successful.

How can someone that is not successful teach us how to become successful? If you want to learn, you must find someone that has already reached success.

You can earn the amount of money you want, but the question is;

HOW MUCH MONEY IS ENOUGH?

? ? ? ? ?

Table of Contents

Introduction	v
First Things First	1
You Must Live Below Your Means	3
What Is a Job	5
Where Do I Start	9
How Do I Improve My Life Style?	21
How Do I Make More Money?	27
How To Keep More of Your Money	41
How To Keep Good Records?	45
How To Always Know Your Net Worth	47
A Warning About Your Money	49
Why Most Businesses Fail	55
How To Avoid Setbacks	59
To Be Led by Your Faith in God	69
Some Of My Accomplishments	73
ABOUT THE AUTHOR	77
Connect with Me:	79

First Things First

What would it profit a man if he should gain the whole world and lose his soul? St. Mark 8:36

There are many things more important than money!

MONEY

It can buy a House………. …..But not a Home
It can buy a Bed……..... …………...But not Sleep
It can buy a Clock…….. …………...But not Time
It can buy you a Book…. ......But not Knowledge
It can buy you a Position………. But not Respect
It can buy you Medicine…………. But not Health
It can buy you Blood…………………… But not Life

So, you see, money isn't everything. And it often causes pain and suffering.

What good is money, if we lose the love of our family?

What good is money, if we live in fear of losing it?

We must keep everything in perspective.
We must share our time with many things;
Family Time.
Volunteer time to make a better community for our family to live in.

Worship time to know that we are accountable to a higher power.

Work to provide for our family.

We must guard against being selfish.

We must realize that we cannot get by without others.

There is a way to make more money and to be honest at the same time.

You should back away from any deal that is not a "Win-Win" situation for all parties involved.

When the day is over, you must be able to go to bed and drop off to sleep without any feelings of guilt.

This study is designed to show you how to reach the financial level you choose.

Only you can say how much money is enough for you.

"One dollar or one million dollars"

"The choice is yours"

You must plan today to make a better life tomorrow.

"Money makes a good man better and a bad man worse."

In the next chapter learn how to "Live below your means."

You Must Live Below Your Means

In the USA, most families desire to live above their means, but, if you plan to improve your life, you must learn to live below your means. This does not mean that you must do without, because you can choose the lifestyle you want to live.

What happens to families who try to live above their means is, they do it on credit and never stop to think how much they are paying in interest to be able to live that lifestyle.

If you pay cash, you can usually buy things at a discount and save money on the cost, while saving the total cost of the interest. This is the same thing as giving yourself a raise in wages. You get the same thing; only, this way, you are saving money and you improve your lifestyle, without credit.

Does this mean that you should not buy anything on credit? The answer is "no." Some things probably cannot be bought without credit, home, car, but you should never buy anything, that will be used up - groceries - gas - clothes, that you will not be able to return, if, you are unable to pay for your purchase.

Never pay more for something than it is worth.
There is "Good" debt and "Bad" debt.
Good debt is an investment that is always worth what you owe on it and will go up in value the longer

you keep it. A good example is a house. If it is well maintained, it will go up in value, the longer you keep it.

Bad debt is anything you buy that is going down in value the longer you keep it. An example of this is a new car that loses value the moment you register it because it becomes a pre-owned or used car that loses 5 to 10 % of its value when the papers are completed and each year the value goes down.

It can lose as much as 50 % of its value in two years. I will explain later how to get the most for your money while living below your means.

In the next chapter learn "What is a job."

What Is a Job

It has been said that a J.O.B. stands for "Just over Broke."

A job is a tool to help you reach your goals. It is up to you to choose the job that best suits you.

Many times, people look at an occupation and feel that it does not suit them because of the type of work involved.

Many people like to have a hands-on job because they like to work with their hands.

Many others like to use their brains to work out problems for themselves and other people.

Many like to train others to do the type of work they are doing or have done in the past.

Some like to operate heavy equipment machinery, work inside a factory, landscaping, secretary, carpenter, electrician, bricklayer, plumbing, drive automobiles, drive trucks, engineer of a train, fly airplanes, work for the government, school teacher, minister, doctor, lawyer, police, firemen, emergency worker, office manager and any of the many other occupations you can choose from.

The main thing is to know that all jobs are important. Don't let anyone make you feel that your job is not important.

On some jobs you will stay cleaner than you will on others, but have you been in a restroom and found that the plumbing is not working. It is a very unpleasant feeling, but someone will have to get dirty to clean it up and get it operating again.

Have you been very thirsty and when you turned the facet on to get water, it did not work; someone will have to repair it to get it working again?

A job is the means to receive the money to buy the things you want. The amount of money you receive will depend on the skills that you have that are necessary for you to do the work that you are assigned to do.

If you have no skills you will have to start at the bottom and work up as your skills grow.

You have the option to choose the work you want to do and offer to learn the skills on the job or you may have to attend a school that will teach you the skills you will need for that type of work.

One of the things you need to learn early is that no job is unimportant.

Don't ever cut corners just because no one is looking at your work. In the most beautiful home on the block, most of the work will be covered up and not seen because it is the foundation that holds the house up. If the foundation is weak the house will fall and may cost many people their lives.

I remember a story I heard many years ago that went like this.

A wealthy man told his foreman that he was going out of the country for a few months and he wanted his foreman to build a house for him. He gave him the blueprints and told him where to build the house and that he wanted nothing but the best materials used. He said do not spare any expenses to build the nicest home in the area.

The foreman was given a sum of money that should complete the house and was told if he needed more, he would receive it when he returned.

Money How Much Is Enough

The story goes that the foreman thought that no one would know if he used inferior materials that would cost less and he could leave out some of the braces and use fewer nails and other materials and the money left over he would put in his pocket and no one would ever know.

When the wealthy man returned from his trip, the foreman gave him the keys to the house and at that time the wealthy man returned the keys to the foreman and told him that he had wanted to do something special for him so the house was a gift from him for being faithful to him all these years.

Can you imagine how the foreman felt when that happened to him? Every time he looked at the house, he realized that he could have had the finest house in the neighborhood, but thinking that no one would ever know; now he was embarrassed about what he had done because he had not done his best. He could not sell the house, because if he did, it would come out what he had done and his reputation would be ruined.

I would like to remind you to think of this story every time you perform any work. Always do your best. Don't ever allow yourself to think that I am not paid enough to do better work. You will be advanced by showing that you feel that your job is important. Never stop learning. If you have extra time, ask what else I can do or will you allow me to watch or help on a job that would help me to improve my skills or learn new skills. As you are seen doing jobs that require more skills you will be promoted faster.

If you have no skills you may have to work on jobs that you don't enjoy, but don't allow that to keep you from learning the skills required for the work you would enjoy.

I read a story that said two men went to work with a railroad line crew. Several years later the president of the railroad line arrived at the worksite and as the president stepped off the train, one of the line workers called out to the president to speak to him. One of the other line workers asked, "How do you know the president." The worker said that he and the president went to work at the same time. The worker asked, "If you and the president went to work at the same time, why are you still working on the line and he is the president?" The man said, "When we first started, I went to work for an hourly wage and he went to work for the company."

Don't ever let the money you receive determine the amount of work you do. Always use your best skills and do your very best to make sure that you earn the reputation that you always give more than you receive. Judge the success of your work by the results. NEVER give less than your best. If you feel that your skills are worth more than you receive, talk to your employer and let them know how you feel. If they are not willing or not able to give you an increase, don't be tempted to do less work, look for an employer that can pay for your skills. NEVER, NEVER, NEVER give less than your best.

In the next chapter learn "Where do I start."

Where Do I Start

You must start at the beginning.

You had no control over how your life started, you may have had a bad start, but you do control how your life will be lived now and how it will end.

When I was born, most people would say that I was born into a poor family. While it is true that we did not have the things that many other families had, I do not remember a time that we did not have a place to live and food on the table.

We moved quite often. At one time in my life, we moved every three months. When three months were up you knew it was time to move. We joke about it now and say even though we moved a lot; we missed a lot of good moves.

I attended many different schools during the first seven years of my schooling. One of the schools I attended only had one teacher to teach all the grades and all subjects from the first to the seventh grade.

When I was only ten years old my mother lost her eyesight and my sister took over all the chores at home. My sister married when I had just started the eighth grade. I was the last child at home and the teachers of the school I was attending would greet you at the beginning of the class when you moved from one class to the next and would give you work to do while in their class and your homework assignment and leave the classroom and you would not see them again until the next day for the same routine. Every Friday we would have a test and if you failed the test that was your problem. That school had the history of moving a student up to the next grade automatically on the third year if you failed two years in a row.

I was twelve years old at that time and would have failed the grade if I had stayed in that school (even though I was an A-B student), so I felt that my mother needed me at home more than I needed to attend school all year and fail, so I left school and stayed at home to care for my mother.

About the time I turned thirteen we moved again and this time we moved into a store building that had a store front and a house built in the back. It was my job to keep house and care for my mother while running the store at the same time. My pay for running the store was a soda pop and pack of crackers (or) bar of candy per day.

When I turned fourteen, I was able to get my driver's license and my father bought a panel truck and I would travel over four counties and pick up laundry and dry cleaning and deliver it back to the owners. I had three routes and my pay was three dollars per week.

At the age of fifteen, I was hired to manage a service station, and each week when I received my pay, half of it went for room and board and the other half was left for me to pay for a car and gas to operate it.

When I turned sixteen, I was old enough to get a job in the textile mill and after being there for a while my pay was up to thirty-five dollars per week.

At the age of seventeen, I met the love of my life and we were married at the time of writing this we just celebrated our 62nd year of marriage.

Money How Much Is Enough

After marriage, I realized the need for additional education, so I went back to night school and earned my GED, and then graduated from American College of Finance. I have studied many subjects and still enjoy reading and I have attended many seminars on different subjects of finance and real estate.

It doesn't matter where you are coming from; all that matters is where you want to go. If you want success badly enough, there is nothing that can stop you from achieving it. The only question is: "How badly do you want success?"

You must know where you are now;
How much do you make now?
How much do you owe now?
How much do you have leftover now?
Does your money run out before the month does?
You cannot solve a problem - until - you admit that you have a problem, and then you must know what the problem is.

You must know where you are now before you can decide how to get to where you want to go. There is a way to get there, but you must have a plan and then, "Follow" that plan. Going faster will not help, **"IF" you are going in the wrong direction.**

You must put this information on paper, to be able to see, exactly, what is holding you back, from the things you want.

You must know what resources you already have to work with and what you will need to get to where you want to go. In the United States, the working classes fall into one of these groups. Which group are you in now and which group do you want to be in?

25.0% earn less than	10,000.00
80.0% earn less than	50,000.00
17.6% earn more than	50,000.00
97.6% earn less than	100,000.00

ONLY - 2.4% of Americans earn $100,000.00 or more

This information shows the level of income each one goes through to reach the level that you choose to grow through to reach that level that you choose to stop at or keep growing. It is up to you to choose

"How Much Money is Enough for You"

What class do you fit in?

You Must Circulate Your Money For it to Multiply!

It is said that Mr. Rockerfellow required his sons to keep a record of every penny they spent, even with their weekly allowance.

His rules were to give the first 10% to charity. This is important because you will never be able to build a large amount of wealth if you are selfish. You must learn to circulate your money before it will grow. It is not hard to give away 1 penny out of a dime or one dollar out of ten, but as the amount continues to grow, it is easy to become selfish. To give away one hundred out of one thousand becomes harder because it is easy to begin thinking about what those one hundred dollars will buy, but we must not be tempted to do this. We must remain faithful to the 10% charity rule.

The next 10% should be set aside as your own money to save for a later date.

After the taxes have been taken out of your wages, this is called take-home pay. When you take out 10% for charity plus 10% for your savings, you have 80% of your take-home pay leftover.

This 80% is the money you have to work with, and your budget should be built around this amount. This is where most people get into trouble because they still budget on 100% of their take-home pay and what they have is 120%. That is the reason they stay in trouble because they are spending 120% rather than 80%. They soon are over their heads in debt and don't know why.

Your budget must show 80% of your income and everything you spend money on.

If you have money left over, pat yourself on the back, as a job well done.

You must have more money coming in than going out. When you reach that level, you are ready to move up to the next level.

This reminds me of a story I heard one day of a family that had been poor all their life and one of the sons returned home one day after working himself up the ladder of success and decided to move his mother into a very large home that he felt she deserved and went back to his own life. This was a very good thing her son did, but, the only thing wrong was that his mother's income could not afford this home. She did not have the money to pay for the lights, taxes, and upkeep, so the result was that she lost this home and the one she was already in because her income could not keep up with her new lifestyle.

Many people have had to file bankruptcy because their income could not afford their lifestyle. That is the reason you must learn to live below your means. Once you get this under control, you are ready to improve your lifestyle.

I will show you how to improve your lifestyle, but the first thing we need to do is to get your budget under control.

You must be realistic. You cannot spend more than you make, without getting into deep trouble.

There are basic things that we need, home, food, utilities, furniture, automobile, clothing, but there are ways to control your spending.

If your house payment is more than 30% of the spendable 80%, you will run into trouble.

You may need to look at good pre-owned cars and furniture to stay within your budget, but if you follow this plan, you will soon be able to upgrade all this to the lifestyle you choose.

You may need to eat more meals at home for a while.

You may need to cook your meals, rather than using the more expensive pre-cooked, pre-prepared meals. Control your utilities - keep doors closed, during wintertime, lower the temperature and wear a light sweater, believe it or not, you will be healthier as a result.

When you get your budget under control, you will be ready to look at ways to improve your lifestyle. You can live better on today's wages.

It's not how much you make, but it's what you keep those counts.

The two largest drains on your budget that you can control now are the interest you pay on loans and taxes you pay to the government.

If you are making payments on loans you have made, you need to look at the interest rates you are being charged.

If you remember, I told you that I married at the age of seventeen and knew nothing about money and how to control it. Back in those days, my wife and I would walk down the street, window shopping and you could buy almost anything you wanted by paying a dollar down and a dollar per week. If we saw something we wanted and I had a dollar on me, we took the item home with us. One day I realized that on payday I would go to town and start at one end of town and by the time I returned to my car all my money was gone until next week when I received my next paycheck, this went on week after week until I worked my way out of the mess, I had gotten myself into.

Money How Much Is Enough

I sat down and worked out a plan to pay my way out of debt. I recorded all of my payments on paper with the amount owed on each one and the amount I had to pay per week on each. I would go to the ones that had the largest balance and ask if I could skip a week and took that money and paid off as many as I could that had a smaller balance and then take the freed-up money next week to catch up on those I had skipped. It took some time but the plan worked and I paid all of them off and freed up some of my money at the same time. If you are experiencing the same problem, the plan will work for you just as it did for me. If you owe credit card debt that has high-interest rates, you can call and ask for a reduction in the interest rate. If the credit card company does not want to reduce your rate, look for a company that offers a lower rate and transfers your balance to that company. Most will charge you a transfer fee; make sure the fee is worth what you will save. Some cards have no transfer fees, look for these cards.

Write down each loan you have and then start with the ones with the highest interest rates and then, if you have several small balances, begin to pay each payment plus extra money, until each of these is paid in full.

If you do not have any extra, you can go to some of the company's you owe large payments to and ask if you can only pay the interest this month and take the principle and pay off some small debts. This will free up some extra money so you can begin to pay extra money each month until all of your debts are paid in full.

You want to reach a point in your budget that will allow you to pay cash for most of your needs. When you reach this point, it will help you to decide if you need something, even if you do not have the money to pay cash. It will help you to decide if this is a "Need" or a "Want."

One day I saw a car that I thought I had to have so I went into the dealership and talked with the salesman and he planned to send me to a finance company and add some of my furniture to the trade-in car that I had, to make the down payment that I needed to buy the car. The words used were a couple of pieces of furniture and after he kept asking me if I had this and that, I reminded him that I had agreed to only put two pieces of furniture on the loan as collateral and he promised me that we had enough to complete the contract. I wanted the car so bad that I did not take the time to figure out what I would end up paying. Not only did I end up with an interest rate of about 50% but when I paid the loan off and received a copy of the paperwork that he had, every piece of furniture I owned plus some that I did not own was listed on that contract. Then I made up my mind that I would not buy anything else on credit other than a house because I knew that I would never be able to save enough to purchase a house using all cash.

This plan worked very well until I found an item that I wanted and I knew that I would not be able to pay cash at that time so I went to the bank and applied for a loan and the loan officer told me that I was turned down because I did not have a credit record on file. After all, I had been paying cash for everything and I had no current credit record. I realized that even though you want to pay cash for most things, it is still important to keep a good credit record on file for the times that you want to borrow for investments that we will talk about later.

You need to keep your money in the bank rather than in your pocket. If you have the money in your pocket, it will be easier to spend. You need to think twice before you write a check to see if this is a need or a want. At this point in your life, you only want to purchase your needs, as your lifestyle improves you will be able to purchase your wants.

After you have all your other debts under control, you need to begin paying down your house, if you already own your house (well, actually, the bank or savings and loan owns your house and you are living in it while making payments to them) (CAUTION) you need to make your regular payments each month and then, ask how much you will need to pay, to pay the principle for next month. You will be surprised to know how little you will have to pay, but the balance that you would have paid is the interest you have saved. Ask for a receipt that says apply to "Principal only."

Remember "PLAN YOUR WORK – WORK YOUR PLAN – If you don't make your plans, someone else will make them for you.

If you have a 30-year mortgage, this is what your payments look like:

$100,000.00 loan, Payment per month $ 733.76, Interest Rate 8%, 30 years

Date	Payment	Principal	Interest	Balance
01-15-00	$733.76	$ 67.09	$ 666.67	$ 99,932.91
02-15-00	733.76	67.54	666.22	99,865.37
03-15-00	733.76	67.99	665.77	99,797.38
04-15-00	733.76	68.44	665.32	99,728.94
05-15-00	733.76	68.90	664.86	99,660.04
12-15-00	733.76	72.43	661.58	99,164.70
12-15-01	733.76	78.18	655.59	98,260.07
12-15-02	733.76	84.66	649.10	97,280.35

Now, look at the above chart and you will see where each payment goes.

When you make your first payment, $67.09 reduces your loan and you own $ 67.09 equity in your home. The bank gets $666.67 plus they still own $ 99,932.91 of the value of your home. If you pay $ 733.76 your regular payment this month and pay the principal $67.54 for the next month, you will save the $ 666.22 interest that would have been due and your ownership equity will increase by the amount of the principal. This is money in your pocket rather than the bank's pocket. The balance owed will be reduced to $ 99,865.37 because you paid before the interest was due. You can keep doing this until the loan is paid in full.

Just be sure to tell the teller that the money is to be applied to the "principal only."

So, you can see that by doing this, you are taking money out of one of your pockets (paying principal) and putting it into another pocket (saving interest while building equity called ownership). As you continue to do this, you will save many thousands of dollars that will be your money, rather than it going to the bank, while you own a larger part of your house with each payment.

When you reach the point that you are following the system and you have freed up part of your money and have more money coming in each month, than you have going out, you are ready to move to the next level.

Remember that you need to have extra streams of income coming in so that if one stream dries up, you still have money to keep you going. I will explain more about this later.

MONEY CHART MONEY EARNED PER HOUR

1 HOUR	8 Hours	12 Hours	16 Hours	24 Hours
$5.00	40.00	60.00	80.00	120.00
10.00	80.00	120.00	160.00	240.00
15.00	120.00	180.00	240.00	360.00
25.00	200.00	300.00	400.00	600.00
50.00	400.00	600.00	800.00	1200.00
100.00	800.00	1200.00	1600.00	2400.00
500.00	4000.00	6000.00	8000.00	12000.00

YOU NEED TO EARN MORE PER HOUR TO IMPROVE YOUR LIFESTYLE

In the next chapter learn "How do I Improve My Life Style."

William T Gillion, Sr

How Do I Improve My Life Style?

You must know what your present lifestyle is and what you want it to be.

You must get your present lifestyle under control. Before you can "safely," change it to a better lifestyle you must ask yourself.

What do you want?
More free time?   **More money?**

How do I move from $15.00 per hour to $25.00 per hour?

Do I work more hours? Do I work two jobs, or do I make more per hour?

Does the company you are now working with, pay more, less, or the same as other companies for the same job you are running? If they pay less, you can move to another company. If they pay the same, you can apply for a position within the company that pays more.

If you are at top pay, then you must look at jobs that pay more.

You must do what is necessary, to increase your "value" to the company.

Most people fall into the trap of asking for a job and accepting the pay that is offered and then complain that they are not paid enough for the job they are doing, so they fall into the trap of just doing what they have to, to keep from being dismissed. This is like sitting beside a fire and saying to the fire that I will give you more wood when you give me more warmth and the fire says that it will give more warmth when it receives more wood. Each blames the other and neither gets what it needs to make progress and without progress, both will wind up in a ditch.

It was said that a worker went to his supervisor and asked for a raise and his supervisor told him that he would relay the message to the Owner. A few days later the worker went back to the Supervisor to get an answer to his request. The Supervisor told him that the Owner said that the request had been approved and his raise would become effective as soon as he did.

You may need to go back to school to learn a new trade that pays more.

If you are married, your spouse could take a job, but if there are children involved, will your spouse make enough to warrant paying someone else to take care of your children?

You must not wait for an opportunity to come to you, you must make it happen.

You should not stop until you can live the lifestyle you want. You must never give up your dreams.

You must control your time because money without time to enjoy it has no value. Here are some things that you can do to control your time.

List all the things that need to be done.
Number them as to how important they are.
What is the value of your time?
What is the value of this project? Can someone else do it at a less pay scale?
Use your time on projects that need to be done by you.

Don't use your time on low pay projects. You must set the value of your time and use it wisely.

Your goal should be; to make the most you can, in the least number of hours, to free up your time, and to do the things that make life better.

Devote quality time with your family

Devote time to charity to improve your community

Devote time to worship to improve your spiritual life

Devote time to develop wealth to offer security to your family

It is not the amount of money that you can make, that controls your lifestyle, but what you do with the money you make and how much you can keep, and how long it takes to make your money (you are looking for ways to "free" up your time).

If you only have one source of income coming in, it will be very hard to improve your lifestyle. I would suggest that you must develop additional sources of income. You must work, but you can choose to do the work you want to do, and then, you must get; your money, other people's money, and other people helping you to achieve the goals you want to reach. Remember, you control the amount of money you have to work with.

MONEY IN: INCOME - Job (Just Over Broke)
MONEY OUT: EXPENSES - House - taxes - car

-groceries - insurance - clothes - furniture -telephone - lights - heat and don't forget 10% charity and your 10%.

You can see how hard it will be to live the lifestyle you want on just one income. And don't forget, if you work for someone else, they choose how much you make and how much time you will have to exchange for your income.

You can see that the more streams of income you have, the easier it will be for you to choose your lifestyle.

Many people fall for the old saying that you need to work for a large company to ensure your security. What I have found is that the only security that you have is the security that you make for yourself. The older generation was told that social security would be all they needed to retire and my parents bought into this myth. I watched my father work at odd jobs just trying to earn a little extra money to keep the money from running out before the month did.

There have been many of my family members that worked all their life in the textile plants in my area and when the plants began to close, they were too old to go back to school and too young to retire and if they did retire, they did not have the money to retain their lifestyle, so they had to accept lower-paying jobs to provide for their families and that also will make their social security checks less when they do retire. Security is only a "myth". The only security is the security you make for yourself, not the security others plan for you. When I saw my father and other family members in this rut, I began at that time to design a plan for my family not to have to face this problem. Remember, you will not make changes until you admit that there is a problem and you see what the problem is. There is a solution to all problems if you are honest with yourself and do not try to hide your head in the sand and hope that someone else will solve the problem for you. This will not happen, because most of the other people have not admitted to their problems.

Security vs. Risk;   Risk vs. Risky

There is more risk or less risk, but you will never develop any security for your family unless you are willing to take a risk. I am not talking about gambling as a risk you should take, but you should always take a risk to "add value" to your life and the skills that you offer to others. As you increase your skills, your value increases and you should look for ways to receive more pay for your increased skills. You control the value of your life and you control how much you are willing to "rent" your skills to others. This is called exchanging your time and skills for money. You have the right to set the fee you are willing to accept. Do not expect someone to pay more than your skills are worth, but don't "sell" yourself and your family "short." You can have anything you want "if" you help enough other people get what they want.

You Must Have a Plan to Improve Your Life.

How much do you earn now?
How much do you want to earn? 2X - 3X – 4X?
What occupations will pay that amount of money?
Choose the occupation you want.
Enroll in a school that will teach those skills.
Seek employment with companies that offer jobs that require those skills.
Don't expect to be paid more than your skills are worth.
Make sure you earn your keep.
Do more than is expected of you.
Seek companies that offer advancement as your skills improve.
If you get a lot of money and don't understand how to use it, it can bankrupt you.

YOU MUST HAVE MORE MONEY COMING IN –THAN GOING OUT

MONEY IN - MONEY OUT

MONEY IN - Income - Job - Two Jobs - Increase in Pay - Wife Work - Investments

Money Out - Expenses - House Payment -car - gro- - ins - clothes - furniture - phone - lights –tax - saving

YOU MUST HAVE MORE MONEY COMING IN - THAN GOING OUT

If you are like most people, you will come up short and you have not learned to live within your means, but, if you have money left over, pat yourself on the back as a job well done. You are ready to move up to your next lifestyle level. If you come up short, you have not learned to live within your means.
"IN THE NEXT CHAPTER LEARN "How to Make More Money"

How Do I Make More Money?

There are at least five ways to make money. You must have more than "one" stream of income to survive today.

You must remember that accidents happen to all people and you must have a backup plan if something happens to you, to keep you from being able to work yourself.

You must have more money going into the bank than there is going out.

Many people try to put more money into the bank, without plugging up the holes that are letting the money out. The less money going out means that it will take less, going in, to have increased.

Money Plan Number # 1

You need to work yourself and don't settle for less than you are worth.

You must look for ways to make yourself worth more,

You must "Increase" your "value" to others.

As you learn to increase your value to others, move from $15.00 per hour to $25.00, to $50.00, to $100.00, to $500.00, per hour, you must keep in mind that you are "TRADING" an hour of your time for every hour of pay that you receive.

You only have 24 hours in a day, and you must take out time for rest to keep your body strong. What good will the money be, if you lose your health, trying to make the money?

You must also control your time. Your time must be used for productive things. Non-productive time is wasted and lost forever.

You must know how much your time is worth and do not use your time on jobs that can be done by someone less skilled and willing to work at a less pay scale.

You must decide what you are willing to exchange for the money you receive. No one will give you something for nothing.

There will come a time when you will need to consider other ways to increase your value, by creating more streams of income. This is the time to find new ways to make money without you having to exchange an hour of your time for the money you receive. This money will come to you even while you are resting or on vacation or devoting time with your family or the many other things you will want to do as your lifestyle improves.

Money Plan Number # 2

The next thing you need to do is to put your savings to work for you. This is the 10% of your income that you set aside for yourself. There are many safe investments that you can place your savings in. Part of this money needs to be available for emergencies, so you do not have to go into debt when the car needs repairs or the refrigerator stops working. As your savings continue to grow, always look for investments that will allow your savings to grow at a faster rate of interest.

This is a good way to increase your value, because you now have a new stream of income, without you having to exchange your time. Your "MONEY" is now working for you.

The only problem with this is that it will take several years for this alone to give you the lifestyle you are looking for, so, you must look for other ways to add income streams to your improved lifestyle financial plan.

If you talk to Financial Advisors, they will tell you that people from every level of income have a problem living within their means. I remember a story that one Advisor told of helping people from high levels of income try to get their finances back in order and one day he looked out the window and saw a friend of his coming in and he knew that this friend was a Minister that chose to minister in the low-income communities and was never paid more than $10,000.00 in a year, so when he saw him coming in, his heart sank because his thoughts were, "how can I help someone that has no income". After their small talk, the Advisor explained that he did not know what advice to offer to help someone with no more income than he had, to rearrange that small amount to clear up his debts.

The Minister then said, "You don't understand why I am here. My parents always taught me to save part of my income, no matter how small it may be, so I have saved $10,000.00 that I have been keeping under the mattress because I don't know what to do with it and I was hoping you could help me to know what to do with it."

If you save 10% each pay period, you will soon be able to have money to invest.

Money Plan Number # 3

The third thing you need to do is find a way to invest "OPM" in other people's money. This is called leverage. What you need is an idea. If the idea is good, other people with money will finance your idea and the outcome will be good for both of you.

(Remember - Win-Win)

Many people choose real estate for this step, as I did because real estate is one type of investment you can make by using "other people's money" to finance your investment. You are furnishing a home for someone to live in that cannot afford to buy their own, and the way you are doing this is by loaning your good name to the bank in exchange for money to buy the house. You collect the rent each month, and after paying the mortgage payment, taxes, insurance, and maintenance on the house, all that is left over is yours to keep, for allowing someone to use your credit.

The investors of the bank are receiving an interest payment for the investment of their savings, the bank is making a profit for loaning you the money that belongs to the investors, you are receiving a profit for your effort in furnishing someone a place to live, and the person that is renting the house has been able to furnish a good secure place for his/her family to live. (Win-Win for all involved)

Not only do you keep all that is left over after the payment and expenses are paid, but every time you make a payment, the amount of the principle of the payment becomes equity or a part of the house that now belongs to you, which your renter paid for you. As time passes, you own more and more of the investment, until you own the house that someone else bought for you.

The good thing about this type of investment is, you can go to the bank as many times as you want to, and the banker will do the same thing over and over because he is looking for good investments for the people that entrusted their savings with him.

There is no limit as to how many houses you can own this way. The only limit is you, if you are willing to use your credit for this purpose and if you don't mind being that deep in debt to the bank. You must remember that the payments must be made to the bank even if the house sits empty.

You must be sure to keep a renter in the house, and if the house is vacant, you must have enough money in the reserve to make the payments. The first one or two houses you buy will be very scary if they become vacant because money is limited at that time, but, as you buy more, there is enough money left over from all of them to keep everything going until the houses are all rented again.

There have probably been more millionaires made through real estate than any other investment, but, don't think that you will get something for nothing, so, you must be able to handle debt, to do this. You can lose everything you own if you do not make your payments on time. It is impossible (for most people) to make money this way without going into debt, but don't forget that this is the "good" debt I told you about.

There are many other advantages to this business. All the expenses, depreciation, plus the taxes and the interest paid on the mortgage are deductions that go on your tax return as a credit to you, even though your renter paid for them all, you get to claim them on your tax return.

Remember, Money must circulate before it can multiply.

I remember when I first moved into the area I now live in, I wanted to buy a house, but, the only problem was that I did not have the money to buy it and I was not known well enough to get a loan, so, I contacted a friend that had some savings in the bank and I approached him about letting me borrow money from him, at two percent interest, above, what the bank was paying him. He agreed to make the loan and I moved into the house. This was a Win-Win situation for all of us, he made more money on his investment, the banker still made his money and I got the house I wanted.

The first rental house I bought was a repossession. I found a bargain house and by this time I had enough equity built up in the house I had bought earlier and borrowed the money I needed to pay cash for this house. The second house was purchased the same way. The next three were bought this way. By this time, I had my credit established to be able to go into the bank and the manager would ask, "How much do you need?" From that point in time, I was able to buy a property with no money down and the loans on the property I bought covered the entire cost and I have even received money back at the time of closing.

I chose to retire early and at this point, my income was coming from my investments and businesses I owned, so, my tax owed, became "0". I found a property that I wanted to invest in and went to the bank and the new manager told me that I would have to furnish tax records for the last two years. Knowing that I had been retired during that time and my income was zeroed out, I told her that I would be glad to furnish them but they may not help. I told her if they understood the Ross XXXX tax system, there would be no problem but, if they did not understand it, the records would not help. After a few days, she called to inform me that I had been turned down because I did not have any income. I went into her office and went through my return and pointed out to her that I had income but I chose to use my deductions to lower my taxes and in this case to "0" out my taxes. She sent this information to the Bank Board Members and in a few days, she called and said, "Your loan has been approved." The next loan I made there were no questions as to my ability to pay.

Money Plan Number # 4

Now that you are working, and have your money and other people's money working for you, it is time for the next step.

You need to put other people to work with you. Every time you allow someone to help you, you will be able to share in the profits made by that person. When you furnish work for others to do, they can support their family. This work can be from many sources when you have reached a level of income that keeps you busy at $50.00 per hour, any work that you need to be done, that can be done by someone in the $15.00 per hour skill level can be passed to them while you are busy at your level of work.

Remember you are wasting your time, if you are doing work yourself, that could be hired out at a lower-skilled rate. You must always reserve your time for the higher paying level.

There are many ways to furnish jobs for others. You could start up a business, but don't forget that you must invest to start it. The type of business will depend on the amount of investment you will have to make. For a franchise business, you can expect to invest from $ 50,000.00 up.

There is no limit on the type of businesses you could start. All you need is a good idea.

The real problem is that you will probably have to invest all that you have plus as much as you can borrow, and you don't know that it will be successful, because many businesses never make it through the second year, without going out of business. Should this happen to you, you will have lost all your investment, so, you must think this through and weigh the cost before you begin. There are many reasons that businesses fail. Just because you are the best in your trade, you must have the ability to do the bookwork, keep up with your taxes, find customers, find the right location for your business, find the right suppliers and find the right distributors for your product, public relations expert and all the other positions that have to be handled. You must be able to do all these things or hire others that are qualified. You must have enough money to keep the business operating until your business reaches the point that the cash flow will keep in step with all other things. Do you have a good source for funds and the ability to repay the loans? Does your credit report reflect the ability to obtain the funds you need? You are buying a job for yourself. Many people have made very good money this way, but many have lost all their money. Most jobs of this type require that "you" work in the business, and most owners work, 12, 16, 18 hours per day. You may make good money, but don't forget about your health, and time to enjoy the money you have made.

Money Plan Number # 5

I have listed this number 5, but it should be listed as number two.

The greatest plan that you will find is the fastest-growing plan today. It is called "NETWORK MARKETING."

Network marketing is the least expensive plan of investment that you will find because someone else has invested in buildings and equipment to furnish work for as many as choose to become a part of the business. You only have to make a small investment to get started and use the supplies that the company furnishes and recommend them to a few of your friends. You have the greatest "Tool of Leverage "that you will find anywhere. You will be in business "for" yourself, but you will not be "by" yourself. You will receive a part of the profit the company makes for every person that becomes a part of the business upon your recommendation and uses the products supplied by the company.

Many millionaires are being made today through Network Marketing and there are many businesses to choose from the investment cost is so inexpensive that anyone can find a way to get started and once you become a part of the system, there is no limit as to how much you can make. This is the best way to learn to operate your own business. If you change your mind, you don't lose everything.

The reason I said that this should have been number two, is that you will not make a lot of money in the beginning, and you will need the income of your job to keep you going until you have time to build this business, but look at all the businesses that start the usual way and go bankrupt or out of business in the first two years without making a profit at all, plus look at the investment they lost.

Most businesses close because they do not have enough capital to keep them going until they start making enough profit to stay in business. In-Network Marketing, the company puts up the capital for the operation and you enjoy the fruits of their investments. There are many Networks Marketing companies in the market place but if you would like to look at the one, I chose, please contact me.

Most people start with money plan number one and work their way to money plan number five, just as I did, but I now know that if I had started with Network Marketing as money plan number two, I would have money to invest in the other things to start the streams of income and still be able to live the lifestyle I wanted to live, while I am enjoying all the other things.

You can choose to work by yourself and keep all that you make, or you can choose Network Marketing and receive all of what you make plus 20% of all the profit that comes from the purchases and sales that each one that you recommend to the company makes also.

Each person devotes 5 to 10 hours per week part-time to recommend the services that the company offers and can you imagine what your part would be when there are 100 or more that are following the advice of you and those that you and they have recommended to the company.

I have done quite well in my planning, but, if I could go back, I would go to Network Marketing earlier.

I must admit that many people do not make a lot of money, but many make big money with these plans. I do not know a better way to learn how to "operate your own business," without making a very large investment. It allows you to see all the hats you have to wear to own your own business, if it is not what you want, you can walk away as many have done and not lose everything you have.

You will learn what you have to do to be successful in your own business.

You will have the same tax write-offs' that big businesses have and as you learn, you will be able to save money on your taxes and decide if your own business is really what you want.

OPPORTUNITY

Henry Ford said, "If you believe you "can" do a thing or you believe you "can-not", in either case, you are probably right.

Every road goes "somewhere," but at the end of some roads is a "dead end."

You must know "where" you want to go before you can choose the road that will take you there. If you don't know where you are going, any road will lead you there. If we don't know where we are going, how will we know when we get there? **If you are going in the wrong direction, speeding up - going faster will not help.**

Things don't just happen; they must be planned. If you don't plan your work "life", someone else will plan it for you.

"PLAN YOUR WORK - WORK YOUR PLAN."

Use the knowledge of others to choose the right road. If you devote a lot of your time driving, working in the yard, cleaning the house, commuting by bus, train, taxi, or airplane, why don't you use this time listening to training tapes or CDs? Let others teach you while you are doing what you do that is non-productive time. Never stop learning, when you reach a level that you can teach others, you must continue to learn while preparing to teach others.

Many people say "OPPORTUNITY" only knocks once, but I say that you make your opportunity.

PROBLEMS "bring" OPPORTUNITY

All people have problems. If you do not like problems, you will never be able to grow to a higher level.

Everything in existence today started as a problem. Someone solved the problem and then others improved on their solution. There is nothing that cannot be improved. That is where opportunity comes in. You should always ask yourself, what "I" can do to improve this item or situation.

Be thankful for problems, because problems make us look for a solution. When we find the solution, we can remove the road block that is keeping us from success. The more solutions we find, the greater our success.

I have coined a phase that says, **"Success is the result of finding a solution to a problem." If you solve enough problems, you will be successful.**

If there were no problems, there would be no reason to search for a solution. Listen to others while they are talking and they will share their problems with you. Take time to make a list of the problems that are shared with you and if the same problem is repeated by more than one person you have found a problem that you can search for a solution and offer to sell the solution on the market.

Any time you see a problem and can offer a solution to solve the problem, you have just found an opportunity to increase your value by helping others to enjoy life more. The more you can help others get what they want, the more you will be able to get what you want.

It was said that a machine was not working as it should, and after the regular repairman was not able to correct the problem, an expert was called in, and the expert, after watching the machine for a short time, took out a hammer and tapped the machine and the machine started working as it should, so, the expert was told to leave a bill for repairs, and the expert left a bill for $200.00 for repairs. Well, the manager was upset because he had seen the expert tap the machine with the hammer, and asked for an itemized bill, so, the expert left an itemized bill that read, tapping with a hammer, $1.00, knowing "where" to tap with the hammer $199.00.

Everyone has knowledge that is valuable to others if we are willing to share our knowledge.

I remember a true story of a man that won $100,000.00 from the local lottery and almost lost his home and everything he owned because he did not know how to handle that much money at one time.

Remember, you will not get anything for nothing. You must decide, what, I will give in return for what I want.

You must change your mindset to be able to quit selling your time by the hour and have your money coming in even when you are not on the job. There are many things that you can do to create a lifetime income without you being present to swap your time for the income.

While I am writing this book, my other income is still coming into me. It allows me to do the things I want to do and enjoy my life at the same time.

Don't let anyone steal your dream!!!

"IN THE NEXT CHAPTER LEARN "How to Keep More of Your Money"

William T Gillion, Sr

How To Keep More of Your Money

One of the biggest expenses you have is taxes.

Most large companies pay little or no taxes. They know how to "ZERO" out.

I heard that Mr. Ross x-x-x-x- never pays over 5% taxes, I decided that I should not have to pay more than he does. He is a multi-millionaire and could afford more, but that is the amount he has chosen to pay, and knows how to time his deductions to keep his taxes at that level. I have been able to do the same thing, even though I am not that wealthy, I do like to use my own money rather than allowing others to spend it for me.

Everyone has the same opportunity to lower their taxes, but most people don't know-how.

Many people complain about the amount of taxes they have to pay, but if you ask them "what are you doing about it" they usually say "there is nothing that I can do." They are so wrong. They think that their tax accountant will take care of them. They take their tax information to their accountant and ask for the forms to be completed for them. That is what their accountant does, complete the forms. Most of them do not know how to lower their taxes, so how can you expect them to know how to lower yours. Just because they are CPAs does not mean that they are experts in the field of work that you are in. You must realize that they are paid for their time just as you are and searching for deductions for you takes time. You must be willing to pay for the extra time they devote to your taxes.

If you do not own your own business, it will be hard, but everyone can afford a Network Marketing Business, and this opens the door for you to use the same deductions as any other business.

If you are self-employed, you can use the same tax breaks that large companies use. You can also use business deductions to lower the taxes owed on the money you made on your employee job.

Everything you buy to be used in or by your business is deductible in some way.

Each dollar you spend on business supplies, allow you to deduct $1.00 from off the top of your business income. You pay taxes on the balance.

When you need an ink pen, pencil, legal pad, stamps, envelopes, desk, file cabinets, bookcases, computer, telephone, answering service, advertisement, use of office space in your home, lights, heating, cooling, automobile (you can deduct the actual expense or the standard mileage which means that for every 3 miles you drive, you can deduct over $1.50 from your taxes). Well, I think you get the picture.

With the right business, everything you do creates tax deductions.

Just make sure that you keep receipts for everything and keep everything legal.

The best way that I have found to keep up with my receipts is to set up a file and give each type of deduction a number and when you make a purchase, take the time on the spot to put the number of the type of deduction so that when you start sorting your deductions you will know where this receipt is to be used.

Some people say, "I don't have the time to keep up with all those receipts."

My answer to that statement is, "The money is yours, but, if you would rather give it away, it is your choice." It is much easier to keep what you already have than it is to make that much extra. "I love receipts because that is money in my pocket."

You control how much money you make and you also control how much you give away through taxes.

If you time your purchases right, you can zero out also. If you need more deductions this year, buy the things you will need next year at the end of this year.

You can also put off buying until next year to group your purchases, to lower your taxes next year if you don't need the deductions this year.

You need to take the time to get a receipt for everything you buy and put a note on the receipt as to what category it will be used in.

The more deductions you have, the fewer taxes you will have to pay.

You must take time to learn what you can claim as a deduction.

Don't be afraid to use deductions as long as you have a proper receipt and it is a legal deduction.

Every dollar you can keep improves your lifestyle because you have just given yourself a raise, by lowing your taxes. If you are in the 35% tax bracket, every dollar of deduction you use, means you just earned 35% interest on your money- not bad huh?

It is easier to keep the money you have made than it is to earn more money, because, you do not have to swap time for this money.

One of the best investments I ever made was to study the tax system. That investment has paid for itself many times over.

It's not how much you make, but it's how much you keep.

"IN THE NEXT CHAPTER LEARN "How to Keep Good Records"

How To Keep Good Records?

You must keep good records.

Devote a little time each day to your records. Work out a system to mark each receipt as to how the receipt will be used to lower your taxes.

Know what your income is and what your expenses add up to.

Timing is everything - you may need to buy in December, if, you need the deductions this year or you may want to wait until January to count it next year.

Do not use a deduction that you cannot prove.

You do not have to worry about claiming deductions as long as you have proof.

Good records are worth their weight in gold.

The study of the tax system is a good investment of your time and money

Don't depend on tax preparers to keep you informed, many tax preparers don't know how to lower their taxes, and cannot or will not, take the time to point out areas in your tax program that is costing you money, which you should not be paying.

Even a tax expert does not understand the entire tax system. An expert is a person that is an expert in a given subject. You need someone that knows about your business and what the tax laws are, that govern the type of business you are in. Many times, even the expert in your type of business may not take the time to keep you informed as to all the deductions you are entitled to, because you must remember that time is money for them also, and unless you pay for the time you use, they may not give you free time.

The more you know about tax laws, will help you to keep more of the money you have earned. I have saved many thousand dollars in preparation fees by knowing what can be used as a deduction in my business. The Internal Revenue Service will not tell you, if, you do not use a deduction you are entitled to use. They only inform you if you use one that you were not entitled to use. They expect you to learn their system and search for your answers. Most large companies pay for lawyers to search through the tax laws for them. You must learn them for yourself.

If You Call the IRS, there are some things you need to Remember

If you call IRS and ask them a question, they will give you an answer, but many times the answer is wrong and if you use the information, they will want to find you for reporting the wrong information.

Be sure to "ask" for the person; <u>name, badge number,</u> and <u>keep a record of the time you called,</u> <u>the day you called,</u> <u>the question you asked,</u> and <u>the answer they gave you to the question you asked</u>.

If they audit you this information will help because they record the conversation and this information will help them locate this information in their computer.

"IN THE NEXT CHAPTER LEARN "How to Always Know Your Net Worth"

How To Always Know Your Net Worth

You must know how much your net worth amounts to.

Don't spend - Invest.
Don't buy anything that goes down in value.
Always have a backup plan.
Always stay in control.
Your net worth must go up each year.
Always keep your "will" current. There will come a time in your investment that you may need to set up Trust Accounts to control your taxes and to control your Estate Taxes.

Enjoy what you have now, and don't let" things" control your life.

Don't let your quest for money keep you from enjoying life itself.

You don't need money to enjoy a sunrise or sunset.

You don't need money to enjoy the waves of the ocean.

You don't need money to enjoy the love of your family.

You don't need money to enjoy the friendship of a friend.

You don't need money to enjoy the love of God.

You don't need money to enjoy the singing of the birds.

"IN THE NEXT CHAPTER LEARN "A Warning About Your Money"

A Warning About Your Money

The **"LOVE"** of money is the root of all evil. I Timothy 6:10

CONTROL YOUR MONEY DON'T LET MONEY CONTROL YOU

The 1st 10% of your income belongs to God, the source of your income.

Take care of your family; I Timothy 5:8 But if any provide not for his own, and especially for those of his own house, he hath denied the faith, and is worse than an infidel.

Always pay the taxes you owe. No more or no less.

Choose the level of income you want or need to live the lifestyle you want for your family.

Seek out what it will take to earn that amount.

Don't become a person that tries to impress others.

Earn your income.

Look for opportunities to have more than one stream of income.

Give to charity as you are blessed, but be careful not to waste or support the wrong causes.

There is a point that money can become a curse, rather than a blessing.

If you live in fear of losing your money.

If you lose the reason for acquiring money.

If money becomes more important than the reason. Your desire to get more money drives you to become the richest person in your city, County, State, Nation, or World.

Money is only paper, if you devote more time trying to get money, than to use it to be a blessing to you, your family, or your community. That is when it becomes a curse rather than a blessing.

You must control your money for it to be a blessing to you. If your money controls you, it becomes a curse to you.

It's not how much money you have; it's what you use it for that makes the difference!

VERY IMPORTANT

Many people keep waiting for the million-dollar income and overlook the double and triple income that is available to them. Just think what that would do for you and your family. Babies start crawling and then start taking baby steps and continue growing until maturity. A million-dollar income is hard to reach, but to double or triple your income with some planning becomes possible. It is possible by taking a step at a time, but to start at the bottom step and jump to the top floor is very hard to do all at once.

Remember:

TIME: Time can never be used again, you invest it, waste it, use it wisely or foolishly, but you only use it once.

You set the value of your time and how it is to be used.

MONEY: It is in your power to choose how much money you will make, how you will make it, and how much is enough for you.

FREEDOM: Freedom is having enough money to live the lifestyle you choose for yourself and your family, having the time to do the things that are important to you and your family at the time you choose to do them.

HEALTH: No amount of money can buy happiness, time, or good health. You must take care of your body by not abusing it. There is also a limit on the number of hours you can go without rest, so it is important to control the number of hours it takes to make the money to furnish the lifestyle you choose.

It is important to protect your health, your time, your money and to use them in a way that would make you a friend to those that you love and to the people you will be around because no one is an island to themselves.

We cannot get along without other people. We need family, friends, business associates, and business clients, to keep our life in focus.

MONEY - HOW MUCH IS ENOUGH THE CHOICE IS Yours

I have started several businesses over the years. Some I still own and some I no longer own. I remember several years ago I owned a sales and service business that had a show window. My son had outgrown some of his toys and asked if he could put some of his outgrown toys in the show window to sell. I agreed and he put several in the window. He had a large "General Lee" like the one the duke boys drove and put it in the window.

A friend of ours worked next door in one of the shops in the shopping center where my business was located. One day she brought her son to work with her, he must have been around six or seven years old. He came down and looked in my show window and saw the "General Lee."

He came down several times before he came inside. After several trips to the show window, he came inside and showed me a penny and asked if he could buy the car with his penny. I told him he would need a quarter and told him to go and ask his mother for a quarter. He came back several times with his penny and I keep sending him back for a quarter.

After several trips, he came back again with his penny and I turned soft and told him he could buy the car with his penny. I knew how much he wanted the car, so I decided to pay the quarter for him and I agreed to take his penny. After he had negotiated the price with me and he had the car in his hand, he started the door and stopped dead in his tracks and looked me in the eyes and asked, "Do I get any change back."

He did not know the value he had negotiated, but he was on his way to learning about finances. I don't know if he still negotiates but he did a good job that time. This is a true story and the moral of the story is even a penny has value. I see many people that do not want pennies in their pocket, but if you don't protect your pennies, you probably won't protect your other money.

The old saying is, **"It takes pennies to make dollars."**

MONEY CHART, where are you now and where do you want to be?

MONEY NEEDED TO EARN PER HOUR TO INCREASE YOUR LIFESTYLE

The chart below is designed to help you to find the amount of income you need to live your chosen lifestyle.

The plan that you want to follow is to:

Increase the income you receive for each hour of your time.

Decrease the number of hours required to increase your income.

MONEY CHART

1 HOUR	8 Hours	12 Hours	16 Hours	24 Hours
$5.00	40.00	60.00	80.00	160.00
10.00	80.00	120.00	120.00	240.00
15.00	120.00	180.00	240.00	360.00
25.00	200.00	300.00	400.00	600.00
50.00	400.00	600.00	800.00	1200.00
100.00	800.00	1200.00	1600.00	2400.00
500.00	4000.00	6000.00	8000.00	12000.00

"IN THE NEXT CHAPTER LEARN "Why Most Businesses Fail"

Why Most Businesses Fail

Most small businesses are started by people that are skilled in the job they are doing. Many times, they feel that they are passed over for promotions or they feel that they are not paid enough for the services they are doing. Sometimes they feel that they are the ones carrying the load and others are being paid for their work. There are many reasons that a person desires to start their own company.

Most small companies are started by people that have limited income, limited resources, limited skills, limited savings, or all the above.

Most people do not stop to think about all the jobs that have to be done by a small business owner.

Each business has its own needs as to how it is operated.

It has been said that nothing happens until something is sold.

We are all salespersons no matter what business we are in. We sell time, service, resources, merchandise, our service, or our skills.

No matter what you sell, you must have a team to work with you.

You need a good **lawyer** to handle your legal matters.

A good **CPA** to keep your books in order and to keep your taxes in order.

You need a **secretary** to handle all calls coming in or going out.

You need a good **Sales Person** to get orders for your business.

A good M**anager** to keep the operation flowing in a positive direction and see that all work is done on time.

Warehouse Person to deliver the services or to do mail out or whatever it is that your company does.

You need good W**orkers** to keep the orders filled on time for the business to make a profit.

You also need **Someone to keep up with the competitors** to keep your prices in line and to keep current as to the needs of your clients.

You can see that you must be able to hire many people to work with you or you will need to wear many hats. This is the reason many businesses fail. You are skilled in what you do, but there are not many people that can wear all the hats that most companies need to be successful. Even if you are skilled in each of these areas, you can only do one thing at a time. When you are on the phone, you may be getting more work to do, but who is doing the work, while you are on the phone. Everything has to be done to keep the business open, but the only thing that brings the money in is when a sale is made and the money is received.

If you don't have helpers, you must do all the things that have to be done. And either your business work hours are too short to make the money you need to stay open or you have to work 18- or 20-hour days to do everything necessary for the business to be successful.

If you bring in workers to help, not even family members or volunteers will work on a regular job without being paid.

Your team members do not have to work all the time, but they must be available to you when you need them.

Most small businesses fail within the first two years. Around 90% fail within five years. Most fail because the owner is overworked, runs out of money to keep the company open or to expand as needed, doesn't have the right advisors, or just decides that this is not what they want to do.

You must have orders for your service, but remember "No one can sell to everyone!"

You can succeed, but you need other people. You need good advisors, salespeople, managers, delivery people, workers, and clients.

Remember, you are in business FOR yourself, but, not BY yourself.

"IN THE NEXT CHAPTER LEARN "How to Avoid Setbacks"

William T Gillion, Sr

How To Avoid Setbacks

Don't sign contracts until you read them

Do not sign contracts until they are completed and be sure to read them before you approve them.

If you remember, I told you about a car I wanted and did not have enough down payment to buy it. I was trading in my car, but I was told I needed more down payment. After I told the salesman I did not have any more money, he suggested that I go down to the finance company to get a loan for the balance.

While talking to the finance officer, he told me that I could use a couple of pieces of furniture as collateral. He began to ask if I had a stove, my answer was yes. He then asked if I had a refrigerator, my answer was yes. He continued to ask if I had several other pieces of furniture. I stopped him and said, "I thought you only needed two pieces" and he told me that he has enough and asked me to sign the contract and he would finish completing the form later so I would not be tied up all morning.

When I finally paid the loan off, I realized that he had charged an interest rate that should not have been legal, plus after I left, he added every piece of furniture I had in my house, plus many pieces I had never owned.

My advice to you is to know what interest rate you will have to pay, and not just what the payments are. Many people never ask what the interest rates are, they just ask how much are the payments and if they can afford them, they sign the contract. Read the contract and know what you are signing because the contract is legal after you sign it.

Don't lose your credit rating

When I was first married, my wife and I would go window shopping. In those days, you could buy many things for a dollar down and a dollar a week and if we saw something we wanted, if I had a dollar on me, it would go home with us.

After I had obligated all my income, I would go to town when I received my paycheck and start on one end of town and make a circle. When I returned to my car, all my paycheck was gone until next week, when I would do the same thing. I finally got tired of going all week without any money and finally worked myself out of the mess I had gotten myself into; I decided that I would start paying cash for everything I bought. This worked very well, because, if I did not have the money to buy something, I did not buy it until I got the money. This helped me to decide if what I wanted was a "want" or a "need." This helped to control my spending.

I continued to do this long enough to allow all my credit records to become so old that they no longer had any meaning.

I had just moved to a new town where I was not known and I was asked to share in an investment that I wanted to take part in, but I did not have enough cash to invest, so I went to the new bank that I had moved my account too and asked for a loan. A few days later my banker informed me that the loan application was rejected because I did not have a credit record for them to evaluate my creditworthiness.

If you have the cash to pay, you can usually negotiate a better deal, but there are some things that it will be hard to pay cash for, such as houses, cars, and other large investments.

You can build your credit rating by, always paying on time. If you open a new account, make the first payment two weeks before the payment is due and then make the second payment when the payment is due. By doing this, they will report to the credit bureau that you pay better than expected.

If you cannot get a loan, open a savings account, and borrow the money against the savings account, using it as collateral. You can open three accounts in different banks, doing this at each bank, and if you use these banks as references, what better reference can you get to establish your good credit. Don't forget to start paying as I suggested.

Always keep a good credit record. You can get a free copy each year from the three credit bureaus.

Don't allow remodeling

When I bought my first rental property, I did not know anything about renting property. I had some good renters, but I also had some that did not want to pay on time and would give every excuse they could find to keep from paying. After having so much trouble I decided to sell the property.

I first rented it to a renter and he wanted to buy the property, but he did not have any money for a down payment and had ruined his credit. I wanted to sell the property so bad that I agreed to finance the property for him.

Things went along pretty well for a short time and one day he asked if he could remodel the property. He said that since he was buying the property, he wanted to make some changes. Not having any experience in renting property, I went along with him on this idea. He started wanting to skip payments, so he could use the payment money to remodel the property because he did not have the money to do both.

Not knowing any better, I agreed for him to do this. After his payments got further and further behind, I told him that he would have to start making the payments.

He had torn out several walls and had never replaced them. When I finally had to have him evicted, I had to go in and repair all the damage he had done to the property before I could do anything with it. I felt sorry for his wife and children and did not want them to have to suffer because of him, so I did not take him to court. He did not have any money anyway. After I had him evicted, his family told everyone that I had taken advantage of him.

If you decide to sell anything and finance it for the buyer, always make sure that you do not permit to make repairs until they have paid you enough money that you could put everything back in its place, if you run into this type of situation.

Black Balled

A few years ago, I took a job in a machine shop. I was the eighth person hired. The company was moving from the north to the south. I found out later, they were trying to get away from the union. I was hired to be a supervisor, but since the company was in the process of moving and was not able to start up for profit, I was asked if I would be willing to work at minimum wage until they were able to start up most of the shop. I agreed because they assured me it would only be temporary.

The union followed them down south and convinced enough workers to vote to hold an election and force the company to allow them to have a vote to see if the people wanted the union to represent them.

I have never been a member of a union and did not want to join. Then, some of the workers came to me and asked if I would sign a petition to give the people the opportunity to choose for themselves. I did not realize the impact it would have on my future. I told them that I did not want any part of the union but I would sign to help them to have the opportunity to vote, but I would not vote for the union if the vote was granted.

The union gave the list to the company and my name was on the list, so I was "blackballed" and was never raised to the pay that I was promised. I worked for minimum wage as long as I stayed there. After several months, I went to them and reminded them that I was promised a raise after so many months. My raise came, but it was only a 5 cents per hour increase.

At the time I decided that it was time for me to move to another company for another job. I found several and they were ready to hire me until I told them where I was then working. At that point, they informed me that they would call me if they could use me.

About the time I was ready to move out of the county, I had a close friend that told me that the company I was working with, had talked the county council into signing a contract with them, to move to that county and that the county council would instruct all other companies in the county not to hire anyone from that company until they had been away from that company for six months. Not many people could afford to be out of work for six months, including me.

I had to leave that county to get another job because I was "blackballed."

Don't sign anything that you do not want to be a part of.

Keep good records by making a paper trail

A few years ago, I owned a TV sales and repair service shop. I had a client bring his TV in for service. He said that he only wanted it to come on. I checked the TV and did the repairs that were needed to come on, but I called him and told him that he would not enjoy trying to watch it because it had other problems. He informed me that he was not concerned about the other problems; he just wanted it to operate.

When I completed the repairs, I completed the repair ticket and "wrote on the ticket" that all the repairs were not made because he did not want to pay for the other repairs.

A few days after he picked the TV up from the shop, he called and informed me that the TV had not been repaired. I told him that any parts or labor that I had done was covered in his warranty. I knew that the name sounded familiar, and I pulled the repair ticket to see what repairs I had done on his TV. When I pulled his ticket, I realized that he was the one that did not want to pay for all the repairs needed.

When he brought the TV back to the shop, I checked the TV and it was playing just like it was when it left the shop. He told me that he had paid for me to repair the TV and he expected it to be fixed or he would call his lawyer. At that time, I asked him if he had his repair ticket with him and he pulled it from his billfold. I showed him on his ticket that I had informed him that other repairs were needed, but he did not want to pay for them. He went into a rage and informed me that he was going to send his lawyer to force me to make the extra repairs and honor my work.

I informed him that I would love to talk to his lawyer and show him the ticket. As he left, he informed me that I would have to complete the repairs. I told him that I would be happy to complete them but he would have to pay for the additional repairs. He said that he would have another shop check behind my work. I informed him that any shop he took the TV to would charge him to repair it.

Always make sure you keep good records of the conversations you have, and agreements you make. Make sure everything is listed that is important to you and that you have written proof of all contracts, receipts, and other things that may come back up at a later date that you will need to be confirmed.

Record: who, what, where, why, and when

Anytime you talk to anyone about business transactions, make sure you record the name of the person you talked to, the badge number if they have one, the subject you talked about and what was said by you and the person you were talking to, the date of your conversation and the time of the day.

When you talk about contracts, insurance, bank accounts, payments made, materials for work sites, record as much information as you can, so you will have it in writing to refresh your mind, if you need to discuss it again.

When Talking to the IRS

Anytime you call the **IRS** with a question, they will give you an answer, but, if the information is wrong, they hold you responsible for the information they furnished and you will have to pay any penalties that they want to charge you for reporting your taxes wrong. If you have all the information, I asked you to get from them, you should be able to prove in court that they are responsible, because you followed their advice.

Don't pay more than an item is worth

You need to learn the value of the things you will be buying. There are many ways to learn the value. You can window shop several stores, you can look in a consumer magazine, and you can go on the internet and shop prices there. Be sure you compare apples to apples, what I mean is make sure that the items are the same manufacturer, with the same features.

Always let the other person give the price first and then ask for a discount. "NEVER" fall in love with anything except your wife and children. If you fall in love with a house, car, furniture, investments, or anything else, you will wind up paying more than it is worth.

Most things are negotiable. I went into the bank up the street from where I normally bank and asked the banker how much interest I would have to pay if I made a loan with his bank. After he quoted me his rate, I went on down the street to my banker and asked the same question. My banker quoted his rate which was higher than the bank that I had not been banking with. I informed him that his rate was too high because the banker down the street had quoted a lower rate and it shocked him. He then told me that if I wanted to shop prices to go ahead and then come back and he would meet or beat the other banks' rates. I asked him, "Why I should have to go shopping for rates to get the best rate from him." I informed him that I had been faithful to his bank and I expected him to be fair with me. Remember, the banker needs you as much as you need him. You may need the money, but it does not have to come from him.

Sharing Information with A Friend

A friend of mine knew that I had many rental properties and came to me one day with a question. His question was, "how much I should have to pay to get a mortgage transferred." I asked him for the details about the account. He informed me that the seller lived up north and wanted to sell the property. The building and loan company that held the mortgage was the same one that he did his banking with. I asked him why he should pay anything for it to be done. Of course, he was puzzled. I then explained to him that the building and loan company keeps a lawyer on hand to do the work for them. Since they already hold the mortgage and the only thing, they have to do is change the name from the seller to the buyer, and since his credit was already established with them, they should be able to do an "in-house transaction."

A few days later he came running up to me and said, "It worked." He later told me that he had always had to pay at least $800.00 to have this done before.

Always negotiate, the bible says, "Ask and you shall receive."

Lowering your taxes is good, but it affects your tax forms

A few years ago, I studied taxes and began to do taxes for the public. I had always been scared to use deductions and just used the standard deduction.

After studying taxes, I realized that the deductions were made to be used, as long as you can show that they are legal deductions.

One day I read that Ross XX XX never paid more than 5% of his income to taxes because he timed his deductions and used the deductions to lower his taxes. I decided that if 5% is what he thinks is right, I would keep my receipts also. By using my receipts for deductions, my taxes also dropped to the 3.5 to 5% bracket.

When I retired and had no paycheck coming from a job, my taxes zeroed out.

I went into my bank and a new loan officer was in charge. I told her that I had found a property that I wanted to buy and that I need a loan. Anytime in the past, all I had to do was tell them I needed a loan and their question was, "How much." But this time the finance officer asked me for the last two years' income tax forms. I informed her that if she understood the Ross XXXX tax system, there would be no problem, but, if she did not, the forms would not help. She informed me that she did not know about that system, but she still needed the forms.

A few days later, she informed me that the loan application had been rejected, because I had no income. I told her that I would explain the system to her. She took notes and called the information in. A couple of days later, she called and informed me that the loan had been approved.

The first time I was turned down was because I had no credit records. The last time I was turned down was because they thought that I had no income. I have made loans since then and had no problem.

Keep good records and know where to find them. Set up a file cabinet. If you keep them on your computer, be sure you keep a backup file because computers do go down and, in some cases, your files are lost. You must have backup files to recover any lost files.

These are only some of the things you must avoid to be successful.

MONEY, HOW MUCH IS ENOUGH?
"IN THE NEXT CHAPTER LEARN "How to be led by your faith in God".

To Be Led by Your Faith in God

I was raised in a very modest family. My parents committed to God when I was very young. They taught me to always be honest in everything I did. I was taught that I must accept responsibility and be accountable for all my actions. They taught me that I could have anything I wanted, IF, I was willing to work for it.

I have heard people say, "I did not ask to be born and now it is their place to take care of me." Guess what? Your parents did not ask to be born either. I am glad that my parents did not choose to have an abortion. It is an honor to be alive and to be able to live in the greatest country in the world.

I am glad I was taught to put my trust in a higher power. As I was being trained, this meant that my parents, my teachers, my government, my pastor, and my elders should always be looked up to and to learn from them the things that helped me to grow and prepare me to someday be one of those leaders to help others grow in the same way I was raised. I was taught that I should put my trust in all those I have named, but I should compare the information with the Bible and accept the things that agree with the Bible, and pass on the things that do not agree with the Bible. I was taught that God in Heaven is the final authority and all things must be approved by His word or my life is lived in vain.

My wife and I were married at a very young age. We had very little training in finances as most young families do. We made many mistakes as I have already pointed out to you.

I remember when we finally had our eyes opened to what debt was doing to us; I put together a plan to work out of the mess I had gotten us into. I was starting a savings plan to have an emergency fund to be able to pay cash in an emergency rather than have to pay for repairs or buy new items on credit to replace those that had worn out. It seemed that every time I would get a few dollars ahead, an emergency would come and I would have to use money out of my emergency fund and I would have a pity party. I was forgetting that this money was an emergency fund; but I wanted to use it as; "a thing that I want to fund." One day as I was having a pity party about having to use the money on an emergency rather than things I wanted, a voice spoke to me and reminded me that the reason for this fund was to keep from having to borrow for this emergency and go back into debt. My answer to this voice was, "Thank you God for reminding me and helping me to keep my priorities in order." I was able to set up the emergency fund and then began a fund for my wants and to be able to buy things I wanted, out of the "extra things I want to fund" and pay cash for them.

I remember one day I went into a car dealership and told the salesman that I saw a car on the lot that I liked and if he wanted to make a sale and would give me a price that I thought was fair I would deal with him. I told him that he would not have a trade-in to worry about and that I would be paying cash. I also informed him that I was going to buy a car but it did not have to be from him. If he wanted the sale, he would have to offer me a fair price. His first price was offered and I informed him that he must not want to make a sale. He went to the manager and came back with another offer. I told him I could live with that offer if he would include some other things in his offer. He finally agreed and I drove the car home. I feel that each of us received a good offer and each of us got what we wanted.

Always Consult God About Decisions

I have always consulted with God about decisions I was about to make. I asked God to allow things to work out for me "if" the thing I was asking about was good for me and could be used in His plan for my life. I used this plan when I met my wife. We were married and other than committing my life to God in our late teens, it was one of the best decisions I have ever made. I have prayed about some things in my life and they were blocked. My prayers have always been, "God, if this is what you want in my life, allow it the come together, if not, whatever it takes, I ask that you block it." I have had several times in my life that I wanted something and it was blocked, you know me, I had myself a pity party. During one of my pity parties, that familiar voice of God reminded me that, if, I did not want His help, don't ask for it. Of course, I could only say, "Thank you, God."

As time passed and I was working out of the problems I had gotten myself into, I would worry about people owing me money and not paying me at the time they had agreed to pay. I have found that even though the money did not come at the time it was promised, it always came at the time it was needed the most. I probably would have used the money to buy things I wanted rather than keeping the money to pay for the things that must be paid at that time. I have found that late payments that are owed to me always come at the time I need them most. I call that, "showers of blessing from God, when I need them the most."

I must tell you that my faith and trust in God has never failed me and I feel that if you will put your trust and faith in God that you will find that your life will be much richer in all things.

Now, my question to you is:

MONEY, HOW MUCH IS ENOUGH? "FOR YOU"

Thank you for reading my book. If you enjoyed it, won't you please take a moment to leave a review at your favorite retailer?

Thanks! William T Gillion, Sr. Author

CONTINUE TO LEARN: "Some of My Accomplishments."

#

Some Of My Accomplishments

I, William Thomas "Billy" Gillion, Sr. have been privileged to do many things during my lifetime.

Some of these accomplishments are:

Married my beautiful wife, on December 23, 1956.

We celebrated our 60th anniversary in 2016.

We were blessed with five wonderful children.

We were blessed with 16 wonderful grandchildren.

We were blessed with 12 wonderful great-grandchildren.

Ran a country grocery store at age 13.

Drove a laundry and dry-cleaning pickup and delivery service van at age 14.

Managed a gas service station at age 15.

Began textile work at age 16.

Worked as a machinist, T.V. technician, insurance sales, and real estate sales.

Born again Christian, believer, and follower of Jesus Christ.

Ordained Minister of the Congregational Holiness Church, Inc.

Former member of Hopewell Congregational Holiness Church, Saluda, SC.

Former Pastor for Pine Ridge Congregational Holiness Church, Hartsville, SC.

Former Pastor for the Ninety-Six Congregational Holiness Church, Ninety-Six, SC.

Present Pastor for the Chapel of Praise Congregational Holiness Church, Ridge Spring, SC.

Member of the General Committee and served as Co-Chairman of the General Finance Committee of the Congregational Holiness Church, Inc., Griffin, GA.

Secretary for the West Carolina District of the Congregational Holiness Church, Inc. Retired after serving nineteen (19) years.

Member of the West Carolina District Presbytery (CFO).

Member of the Shingle Hollow Campground Committee, Rutherfordton, NC.

Former Owner of Gillion Television Sales and Service of Ninety-Six, SC.

Former Owner of Gillion Tax Service of Ninety-Six, SC.

Former Owner of Ninety-Six Realty Co, of Ninety-Six, SC, President, and Broker-in-charge.

Former Owner of Ninety-Six Insurance Agency, Ninety-Six, SC. CLU, LUTCF Earned Fellow Degree, FLFP, and Certified Instructor.

Former member of National, State, and Local Association of Life Underwriters.

Current Owner of Gillion Rental Properties.

Former National Commander for Royal Rangers.

Former National Royal Rangers Training Instructor/Trainer/Coordinator.

Former Sr. Commander and Founder, of the Fairfax Rescue Squad in Saluda County.

Former member of "SCARS" South Carolina Association of Rescue Squads.

Former member of Ninety-Six Chamber of Commerce.

Served seven years in the South Carolina National Guard (1956- 1963) during Vietnam War.

Past District Deputy Grand Master of the Grand Lodge of Masons of South Carolina of the ninth (9th) Masonic District.

Life Member and Past Master of Travis Masonic Lodge # 241 of Saluda, SC.

Member of the Order of the Eastern Star.
Former Red Cross First Aid Instructor
Former Emergency Medical Tech.
I taught the first "CPR" class in Saluda County

before it was approved by the (AMA). American Medical Association.

Former Electronics Instructor, Piedmont Technical College Greenwood, SC.

Former Business, Finance, Insurance, Instructor, Piedmont Technical College.

Completed the Constitution 101 course with Hillsdale College.

Former airplane pilot.
Singer
Musician.
Songwriter.
Former Saluda County Republican Party

Chairman.

Higgins / Zoar Poll Manager, Saluda, SC
Centennial Poll Manager / Clerk, Saluda, SC
Named to Business "WHO'S WHO."
Drove one time on dirt race track Greenwood, SC.
Drove one time on NASCAR race track at

Darlington, SC.

Valedictorian of several classes taken at Piedmont Technical College of Greenwood, SC.

Author/Publisher books:

Money-How Much is Enough

Walking Down Memory Lane

Christian Growth-Leader Edition

Christian Growth-Student Edition

They are available at most major book stores.

The family burial spot is at Hopewell Congregational Holiness Church, Saluda, SC.

CONTINUE TO LEARN: "About the Author."

# # #

ABOUT THE AUTHOR

William T Gillion, Sr. has been involved in business transactions from the age of five. We lived on a farm and we would pick vegetables and put them in a farm wagon and park the wagon beside the road and sell the vegetables to people passing by. We left the farm after that and moved into town. Houses were being constructed close to where we were living and we took my small wagon and a washtub and put ice and soft drinks and candy and crackers to sell to the construction workers at lunchtime. After the construction was completed, I used my lawnmower to cut grass for those in our community.

I am now semi-retired and cut back on my business, but over the years I have owned several businesses: A small country store, TV sales and service, Tax service, Insurance Agency, Used Car Sales, Owner and Broker in charge of Real Estate Office and Rental Properties. I still own the Rental Properties but have sold most of the other businesses.

I have learned quite a lot from the businesses and I want to share this knowledge with you to help you to reach the level of income and the lifestyle you choose, without making a lot of the mistakes I made.

William T Gillion, Sr

Please visit your favorite book retailer to discover other books of knowledge that have been written by William T Gillion, Sr.

Go to the next page to "Connect with me."

Connect with Me:

Here Are My Social Coordinates:

Favorite my "Amazon.com" author page:

Friend me on Facebook: http://www.facebook.com/williamgillion

Tweet me on Twitter: http://twitter.com/williamgillion

For questions or comments: Send Email to: booksbybillyg@outlook.com

Check out my current Books that are available to sample, buy and give copies as great gifts.

Money-How Much is Enough: https://www.amazon.com/dp/1796515220

Walking Down Memory Lane: https://www.amazon.com/dp/172009506X

Please visit your favorite book retailer to discover books by William T Gillion, Sr.

I appreciate you reading my books.

Please remember to leave a review for my books at your favorite retailer.

#

William T Gillion, Sr

Money How Much Is Enough

www.ingramcontent.com/pod-product-compliance
Lightning Source LLC
Chambersburg PA
CBHW020600220526
45463CB00006B/2392